CHILDREN
OF THE
BIBLE

CARINE MACKENZIE

© 1993 Christian Focus Publications

ISBN 1 857920325

Published by
Christian Focus Publications Ltd
Geanies House, Fearn, Ross-shire,
IV20 1TW, Scotland, Great Britain.

Illustrations by William Geldart
Text by Carine Mackenzie

Printed and bound in Singapore

Contents

Children Of The Old Testament

Children are important to God. He loves them and takes care of them.

In the Old Testament we read about boys and girls who loved God. Some were important and became kings; some were brave and became soldiers; others were servants or prisoners.

God wants us to know about each one of them and to learn from them. As God took care of them in difficult situations, so he will take care of us. We must remember to ask him to help us.

"Remember your Creator in the days of your youth."

Ecclesiastes 12:1

Isaac - Child of Promise

Genesis 21

Isaac was born when his parents, Abraham and Sarah were very old. God told Abraham that Sarah would have a child, and he laughed in astonishment. When Sarah overheard angels tell Abraham again that his wife would have a baby, she laughed too. It seemed so impossible but it was in God's plan that Abraham and Sarah should have a son.

Just as God had said, Sarah gave birth to a baby boy. God told Abraham to call him Isaac, meaning 'Laughter'. Probably Abraham and Sarah would always be reminded of the fact that they laughed in disbelief at God's promise of a son.

Young Isaac gave a lot of pleasure to Sarah and Abraham in their old age. He brought laughter and happiness to their home. When he was about two or three years old Abraham had a big party in his honour.

Ishmael - Sent Away

Genesis 21

Everyone was happy except Sarah. She was jealous. Abraham had another son, Ishmael, who was now a teenager. His mother was Hagar, Sarah's maid. Sarah was afraid that Ishmael would take Isaac's rightful place and inherit God's promises. She felt that Ishmael was making fun of young Isaac.

"Get rid of that slave woman and her son," she told Abraham. "That boy will never share the inheritance with my son Isaac."

Abraham was upset by Sarah's words, but God told him not to worry.

"Do what Sarah says," said God. "It is through Isaac that your family will be blessed but I will look after Ishmael, because he is your son. I will make his family a great nation too."

Early next morning Abraham took some food and water and gave them to Hagar. He sent her away into the desert with Ishmael to look after themselves.

Ishmael lay down under the shelter of a bush feeling so thirsty. Hagar moved a little way off.

"I cannot watch him die," she sobbed.

God heard them both crying and spoke to Hagar.

"Do not be afraid. Take Ishmael's hand and lift him up. I am going to make him the head of a great nation."

God opened Hagar's eyes. She saw for the first time a well of water nearby. She quickly filled up the skin bottle and gave Ishmael the drink that he so badly needed.

God continued to look after Ishmael. He lived in the desert, hunting for food with a bow and arrow.

Isaac - God Provided

Genesis 22

God had promised Abraham that Isaac would be the one to continue the family line. One day he tested Abraham's faith. God called to Abraham.

"Take your only son, Isaac, whom you love and go to Moriah," said God. "Sacrifice him there as an offering on the altar."

How could Isaac be a father of a great nation now? But Abraham remembered that with God all things are possible so he set about obeying God's instructions.

Early next morning Abraham saddled his donkey and cut a large bundle of wood. Taking Isaac and two servants, he travelled to Mount Moriah.

As they went up the hill together Isaac felt puzzled.

"We have the fire and the wood here," he said, "but where will we get the lamb for the burnt offering?"

"God will provide the lamb," replied Abraham.

So the father and son continued to climb the mountain.

When they came to the right place; Abraham built an altar and arranged the fire-wood on it. He tied Isaac's hands and feet and laid him on the altar. Abraham believed that God was in charge. He raised the knife in his hand. Then the angel of the Lord called out to him, "Abraham, Abraham!"

"Here I am," he replied.

"Do not harm the boy," he said. "Do not do anything to him. I know that you fear God because you were willing to sacrifice your only son."

Just then Abraham looked up and he saw a ram caught by its horns in a bush. This animal was used as the sacrifice for a burnt offering. God had provided the lamb for the sacrifice.

An angel spoke to Abraham again, telling him that God would bless him and his family.

How glad Abraham and Isaac would have been as they returned home.

Joseph - The Dreamer

Genesis 37

Joseph lived with his father Jacob and eleven brothers in the land of Canaan.

Joseph was his father's favourite. He loved him more than any of the other boys.

When Joseph was seventeen years old, Jacob gave him a very special ornamental coat. The other brothers were jealous when they saw it. They would not say a kind word to Joseph.

One night Joseph had a dream and the next morning he told it to his brothers.

"We were all binding sheaves of corn out in the field. Suddenly my sheaf rose and stood upright, while your sheaves gathered round and bowed down to it."

The brothers disliked him all the more.

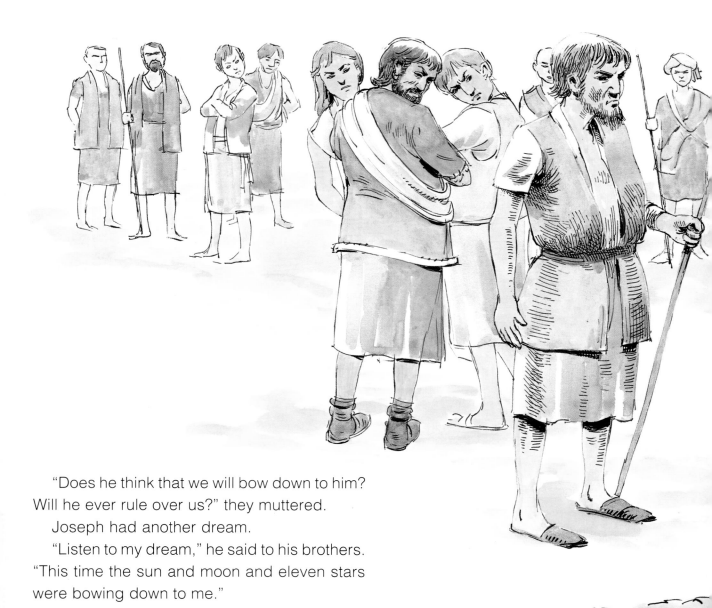

"Does he think that we will bow down to him? Will he ever rule over us?" they muttered.

Joseph had another dream.

"Listen to my dream," he said to his brothers. "This time the sun and moon and eleven stars were bowing down to me."

When he told his father too, Jacob rebuked Joseph. "Surely you do not think that I and your mother and brothers will actually bow down to you, do you?"

His brothers really hated Joseph.

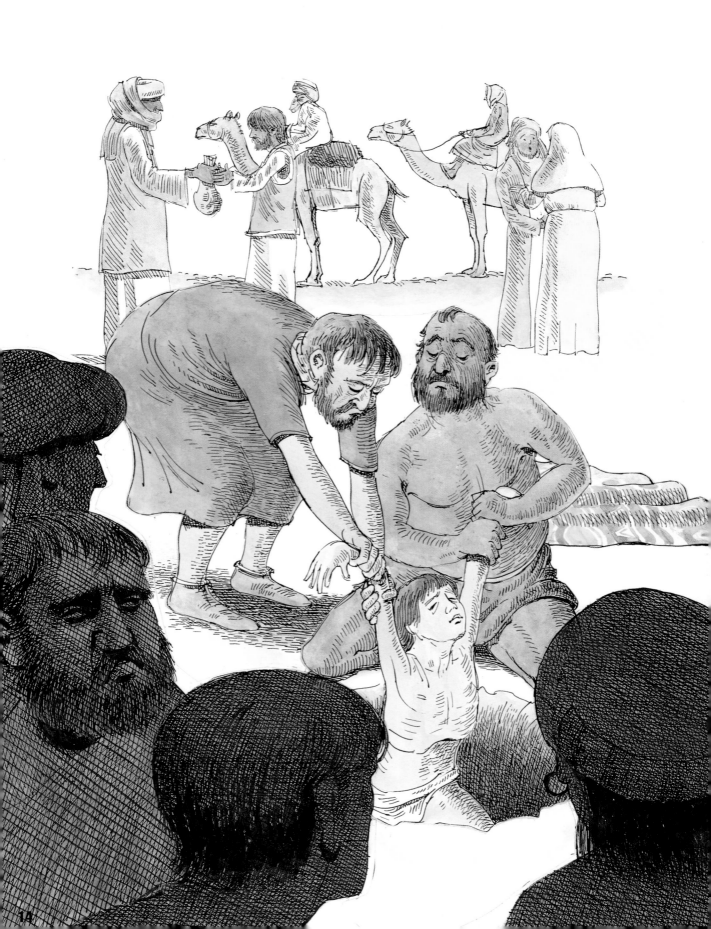

Joseph - Sold to Egypt

Genesis 37 & 45

One day Joseph's father said to him, "Go out into the country where your brothers are looking after the sheep. Find out if they are all well and come back and tell me."

Joseph willingly did as his father asked him. The brothers saw Joseph coming.

"Here comes that dreamer," they grumbled. "Let's kill him and drop him into a pit. We can say a wild animal ate him. Then what happens to his dreams?"

Reuben, the eldest spoke up.

"Let's not kill him. Throw him into the pit but don't hurt him." Reuben's plan was to rescue him later and take him back home.

When Joseph came to greet his brothers they grabbed him and pulled off the beautiful coloured coat. Poor Joseph was tossed into the pit. How horrible to be in the dark, dirty pit all alone.

A group of merchants came along. Their camels were laden with spices and perfume to sell in Egypt.

"Let's sell Joseph to these merchants," suggested Judah. "He is our brother after all. We had better not kill him." The others agreed.

So Joseph was sold for twenty pieces of silver and taken off to Egypt to work as a slave.

Reuben was distressed when he found Joseph gone.

"What can we do now?" he asked.

A plan was hatched to deceive Jacob. They killed a goat and dipped Joseph's coat in its blood. When they reached home they showed the blood-stained coat to Jacob who knew it belonged to Joseph.

"He must have been killed by a wild animal," he thought. He mourned for his son Joseph and could not be comforted.

The Lord was with Joseph through all his difficulties. He was a slave in the home of a high official and pleased his master. Then, one day he was wrongfully accused and thrown into prison.

God had a plan for Joseph. King Pharaoh heard that he could understand the meaning of dreams and asked Joseph to explain his dreams. With God's help Joseph was able to tell Pharaoh to prepare his country for a long severe famine. Joseph was asked to look after the food supplies.

Years later some men from the land of Canaan came to Egypt to buy food. They bowed down before this important man whom they did not recognise, asking for his help. Joseph's dream had at last come true. Joseph did not try to get revenge. He saw God's purpose in his life.

"You meant to do me harm," he said to them, "but God meant it for good."

Moses - Baby in the River

Exodus 2

Pharaoh king of Egypt hated the Israelite people who lived in his country. He was afraid that they would become strong and powerful and might fight against him one day. He put slave masters over them and forced them to work hard for him. He gave a cruel order.

"Every boy that is born to an Israelite mother must be thrown into the river Nile."

One day a baby boy was born to an Israelite couple, Amram and his wife Jochebed. They hid him in their house until he was three months old without the Egyptian people knowing he was there. As he grew bigger and noisier it was not so easy to hide him. So Jochebed thought of a good plan. She made a basket of reeds, and made it waterproof by coating it with tar and pitch. She put her young baby into the basket and hid it among the reeds along the banks of the river. His sister Miriam stood a short distance away to see that he was safe.

Pharaoh's daughter, the princess, came down to the river to bathe. As she walked along the river bank she spotted the basket. Her servant girl was sent to fetch it. The basket was opened and there lay a little baby, crying. The princess felt so sorry for him. "This must be one of the Israelite babies," she exclaimed.

Miriam came out of hiding and went to speak to the princess.

"Shall I go and get one of the Israelite women to nurse the baby for you?" she asked.

"Yes, go," replied the princess.

Miriam ran home and fetched her mother.

"Take this baby and look after him for me. I will pay you," the princess told Jochebed.

There was no need to hide the baby now. The princess called him Moses which means 'Drawn out' because she had drawn him out of the water.

God had kept Moses safe because he had a plan for his life. When Moses grew a little older, he went to live in the palace where he was educated like a prince. He always remembered that he was an Israelite and he worshipped the true God.

Children - Wanting to know

Deuteronomy 6 & Joshua 4

Moses became the leader of the people of Israel. He took them on a long journey from Egypt to Canaan, the country that God had promised to give them. God gave them rules for living, called the Ten Commandments.

These rules were not just for the adults but for the children too. The mothers and fathers were specially asked to teach these rules to their children - to talk to them about God's law as they sat at home or when they were walking along the road, when they went to bed at night and when they got up in

the morning. It was very important for the children to know God's word.

God guided the Israelite people across the river Jordan into the land of Canaan. The river miraculously stopped flowing to allow everyone to cross the river bed on dry ground. Twelve strong men were told to pick up a big stone from the middle of the river bed and carry it over to the camp. There they built them into a monument. This was to be a reminder of God's care over them. In days to come the children would ask "What do these stones mean?"

The parents would then tell the children how God stopped the waters of the river Jordan flowing to allow the people of Israel to pass over on dry land. They should never forget how God cared for them.

Samuel - The Boy God spoke to

1 Samuel 1& 3

Hannah was a very sad woman. Her husband loved her very much but Hannah had no children. She was so unhappy, she wept all day and would not eat.

Hannah went to the temple to pray about her problem. She begged the Lord to give her a son. She promised she would give him to God to work for him all his life. Eli the priest comforted her with the words, "Go in peace. May God give you what you have asked."

Hannah cheered up and felt like eating again. She went back home with her husband. In time she gave birth to a baby boy. She called him 'Samuel' which means 'asked of God'. She had asked God for a baby and God had answered her prayer.

Hannah enjoyed looking after her little boy. When he was old enough she kept her promise to God. She took him to the temple at Shiloh and left him there to work in God's house with Eli the priest.

Every year his mother and father would come to the temple to worship. Hannah brought a new coat for Samuel each time she came. God was pleased with the work he did in the temple.

One night Samuel was lying on his bed in the temple. He heard a voice calling his name, "Samuel."

"Here I am," Samuel answered, running through to where Eli was lying. "Here I am, you called me."

Eli replied, "I did not call you; go back and lie down."

Again the voice called "Samuel!" He got out of bed and went to Eli. "Here I am; what do you want?"

"My boy, I did not call you," repeated Eli. "Go back to bed."

The voice called "Samuel" a third time. Once more Samuel went through to Eli. "Here I am. You did call me."

Eli then realised that the Lord was speaking to Samuel.

"Go and lie down," he told Samuel. If he calls, say 'Speak Lord for your servant is listening.'"

Samuel went back to his bed. Once more the Lord called Samuel's name.

"Speak for your servant is listening," he replied.

God spoke to Samuel, telling him how Eli's wicked family would be punished, and Eli too because he had not tried to correct them. The next day Samuel was afraid to go and tell Eli what God had said. Eli called him in. "What did God say to you?" he asked.

Samuel told him everything. Eli accepted all that Samuel said. "He is the Lord," he said. "May he do what pleases him."

God was with Samuel as he grew up and he became a prophet. God spoke to the people through him.

David - The Shepherd Boy

1 Samuel 16

David was a shepherd boy who looked after his father Jesse's sheep. He was the youngest in the family, healthy and handsome. One day Samuel the prophet arrived unexpectedly at Jesse's home in Bethlehem. The purpose for his visit was to choose a young man from this family who would be anointed as the next king of Israel.

When Samuel met David's eldest brother Eliab, he thought he was a fine person. "Surely this is the one the Lord will choose."

"This is not the one," said the Lord. "Looks are not the most important thing. God sees the heart."

Abinadab, the next son then met Samuel, but he was not the right one either. Shammah was also rejected. One by one Jesse's sons came up to Samuel. Each time Samuel had to say, "The Lord has not chosen him."

"Are these all the sons you have?" he asked.

"There is still the youngest one," replied father Jesse. "He is looking after the sheep."

"Send for him," said Samuel.

David was brought in from the hill-side to meet Samuel.

"Anoint him," the Lord told Samuel. "He is the one."

Samuel took the container of oil and anointed David in front of all his older brothers.

One day he would be the king!

The king at that time was called Saul. Once, when he was very depressed his servants suggested that pleasant harp music might make him feel better.

"Find someone who plays well, and bring him to me," ordered Saul.

"One of Jesse's sons plays the harp. He is a fine young man. The Lord God is with him," the servant answered.

David was summoned to the king. Saul liked David very much: he wanted him to stay all the time. Whenever Saul felt bad, David would play beautiful music on his harp and Saul would feel much better.

David Beats Goliath

1 Samuel 17

David's three eldest brothers were soldiers in Saul's army. The army was at war against the Philistines who had a giant warrior, called Goliath fighting for them. All the Israelite soldiers were terrified of him.

Jesse was worried about his sons in the army. "Go and see how they are getting on," he said to David one day. "Take some food for your brothers and some cheese for their commander. Bring me back good news."

David set off early and reached the camp as the army was going out to battle. He left the food with the man in charge of supplies and ran to find his brothers. Just then Goliath stepped out from the Philistine army and shouted insults at the Israelite army. All the soldiers ran away in fear.

"Who does he think he is, defying the army of the living God?" asked David?"

Eliab, David's eldest brother was very annoyed with him. "Why did you come here? Just to watch the battle, I'm sure. You should be looking after your sheep."

"What have I done now," replied David. "Am I not even allowed to speak."

Saul heard that David was in the camp and sent for him. David said to Saul "Don't let anyone be afraid of this Philistine. I will go and fight him."

"You are only a boy," said Saul, "and he is a trained soldier."

"I have some experience of fighting," answered David. "When a lion or a bear would attack my father's sheep, I would go after it and rescue the lamb and kill the wild animal. God who helped me to kill the lion and the bear, will help me to kill Goliath."

Saul did not have anyone else willing to fight the giant. He decided to let David try.

Saul gave David his own armour to wear but David could hardly move in it. He was not used to it, and decided to do without it. He took his shepherd's staff, picked five smooth stones from the stream and put them in his shepherd's bag. His sling was at the ready in his hand.

When Goliath saw David coming, he could see that he was only a boy. He started shouting insults.

"I'm coming to you with the help of the Lord Almighty, the God of the armies of Israel," shouted David. "The battle is the Lord's; he will give all of you to us."

David ran forward, took a stone from his bag, put it in his sling and took aim. The stone hit Goliath on the forehead and he dropped dead. David ran up

to Goliath's body, took his sword from its
sheath and cut off his head. When the
Philistines saw what had happened to their
champion fighter they turned and ran. The
Israelites ran after them chasing them away.
    David was a hero.
    He had beaten the
Philistine warrior with
God's help.

The Boy who was hungry

1 Kings 17:7-24

There was a very bad famine in Israel.

No rain had fallen.

The streams had dried up.

The crops had failed.

Elijah was hungry. He was one of God's messengers, who told the people God's word.

God spoke to Elijah. "Go to Zarephath. I have told a widow there to feed you."

When Elijah reached the town, he met the widow out gathering sticks.

"Would you bring me a little water to drink?" he asked her. "And a piece of bread, please."

"I don't have any bread - only a handful of flour and a little oil. I am just gathering these few sticks for the fire, so that I can bake a loaf for myself and my son. After that, there is no food left. Then we will starve to death."

"Don't be afraid," said Elijah. "Go home and bake your loaf, but make a little cake for me first. God has told me that your flour will not be used up nor will your oil run dry, until the drought is over."

God miraculously provided for them so that there was plenty of food every day for the widow, her son and Elijah.

Later the boy became sick. His illness was so bad that he died.

"Why did this happen to us?" the woman asked Elijah.

"Give me the boy," replied Elijah.

He carried him upstairs to his room, and laid him on the bed. He stretched himself out on the boy's body and begged God three times to bring him back to life.

God heard Elijah's prayer and the boy began to breathe again. Elijah carried him back downstairs to his mother.

The woman then realised that Elijah was a man of God, who spoke the truth.

The Boy who came back to Life

2 Kings 4:8-37

Elisha was a man of God. He travelled round Israel telling God's word. When he came to Shunem he would stop for a meal in the home of a rich couple. One day the lady said to her husband, "Elisha is a man of God. Let's make a little room for him, with a bed, a table, a chair and a lamp. He can stay there whenever he visits us."

On one visit Elisha asked his servant Gehazi to fetch the lady. "You have gone to so much trouble for me. How can I repay you? Can I speak to the king for you.

"No," replied the woman. "I have a good home. I do not need anything?"

"What can I do for her?" Elisha wondered.

"Well," said Gehazi. "She has no son, and her husband is old."

"Call her back," ordered Elisha.

As she stood in the doorway, Elisha gave her this amazing news. "About this time next year, you will be holding your own baby in your arms."

"Oh no, don't tease me," she said.

But Elisha's words were true, and a year later she gave birth to a lovely baby boy.

The little boy grew strong and fit. One morning he was out in the fields with his father at harvest time watching the reapers at work. Suddenly he called out "My head! My head!"

"Carry him home to his mother," his father told a servant. The little sick boy sat on his mother's knee until noon and then he died. The heart-broken mother carried him upstairs to Elisha's little room and laid him on the bed. She shut the door and went out to find her husband.

"Please give me a donkey and one of the servants. I have to find Elisha the man of God."

Elisha noticed the lady coming in the distance. He sent his servant to meet her to find out what was wrong, but she would not confide in him.

When she reached Elisha she fell down at his feet. "Did I ask you for a son, my lord?" she cried. "Didn't I tell you not to raise my hopes?" Elisha then realised that something had happened to the boy.

"Run as fast as you can, Gehazi. Put my stick on the boy's face," said Elisha.

"No," said the boy's mother. "I am not going to leave until you come yourself."

So Elisha came too.

Gehazi reached the house first but when he put Elisha's stick on the boy's face, nothing happened.

As soon as Elisha reached the house, he went up to his room and shut the door. He prayed to the Lord. Then he lay on top of the boy on the bed, mouth to mouth, eyes to eyes, hands to hands. Soon the boy's body grew warm. Elisha paced up and down in the room. Once more he stretched himself out on top of the boy.

This time the boy sneezed seven times and opened his eyes. God had answered Elisha's prayer and brought the little boy back to life.

How thankful the mother was to have her little boy alive again.

The Girl who helped her master

2 Kings 5

A little Israelite girl was taken captive by an invading army to a foreign land. She had to work there for the wife of Namaan who was a leader in the army. Naaman was wealthy and important but he had a very serious skin disease called leprosy. He had not found a cure and would have to leave his wife and home one day as the disease was very infectious. Naaman and his wife were very sad.

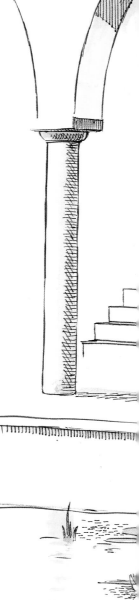

One day the little girl said to her mistress, "If only the master would go to see the prophet of God who lives in Samaria. He would cure his illness."

This suggestion was passed on to Naaman. He lost no time in making arrangements to go to Samaria. Elisha the prophet heard about him and called for Naaman to come to see him. Elisha gave some strange advice. Naaman was to wash seven times in the river Jordan. The very idea disgusted him. "I have better rivers at home," he grumbled. "Can he not do better than that?"

His servants persuaded Naaman to obey Elisha.

"Wouldn't it be quite easy just to do as he says and see what happens?"

At last Naaman agreed. When he came out of the river the first time, nothing was different; the second and third times still the leprous spots were showing.

"I knew this wouldn't work," thought Naaman. He came out of the water for the fourth time and he was no better. Surely this was hopeless. Was it worth trying any more? Into the water went Naaman for a fifth time and then a sixth time and still his skin was as bad as ever. He would try it just once more. When he came out of the river for the seventh and last time, his skin was completely better, as fresh and smooth as a young child's. What a miracle!

Naaman was delighted. He went back to Elisha and confessed, "The God of Israel is the only true God."

How delighted the little girl must have been when her master Naaman came back home cured from his terrible disease.

Joash - The Boy King

2 Kings 11 & 2 Chronicles 22

Joash was the son of Ahaziah, king of Judah. Ahaziah was a bad king; he did not love and serve God. He was killed by his enemies when Joash was just a baby.

When Athaliah, Joash's grandmother, heard that Ahaziah was dead, she decided to kill all the royal family, including Joash.

Joash's aunt Jehosheba took him away secretly and hid him with his nurse in a bedroom in the temple. Jehosheba and her husband, Jehoiada the priest, looked after Joash carefully for six years. He was the rightful king but his grandmother had made herself queen instead.

Jehoiada made a plan to put Joash on the throne. He sent for the commanders of the army and asked them to stand guard with all their men at the temple. Jehoiada brought the seven-year-old Joash out of the temple, put the crown on his head and announced that he was the king. He was anointed with oil, the people clapped their hands and shouted "Long live the king."

When Athaliah heard all this noise, she hurried over to the temple. There she saw Joash standing by a pillar with the king's crown on his head. "Treason! Treason!"

she screamed, tearing her clothes in fury. Jehoiada ordered the soldiers to grab her. The evil queen was quickly seized and put to death. Joash and the people had nothing to fear now because Athaliah was gone.

Joash reigned in Judah for forty years. He was a good king with the help and teaching of Jehoiada the priest.

Children of the New Testament

The most important child we read about in the New Testament is the Lord Jesus. We learn of his miraculous birth and his sinless life.

Jesus loved children and he talked with them and watched them at play. He used them to teach grown-ups lessons about humility. He blessed them and prayed for them. Several times he healed children who were very ill and even restored some to life.

Young children were able to work for him and to praise him.

Jesus said "Let the little children come to me, and do not hinder them for the kingdom of heaven belongs to such as these."

Matthew 19:14

The Girl raised to Life

Luke 8:40-56

Jairus and his wife had an only daughter who was twelve years old. Jairus was an important man in the church. He was sad. His daughter had become very ill. 'Perhaps Jesus will help,' thought Jairus. He left the little girl at home with her mother and went to find Jesus. When he met him, he fell down on his knees and begged Jesus to come to his home to help his daughter.

On the way Jesus stopped to heal another sick lady. Poor Jairus waiting for Jesus! Why would he not hurry?

Then a message came from Jairus' home. "Your daughter is dead. Don't bother Jesus any more."

Jesus overheard this remark. "Don't be afraid," he said to Jairus. "Just believe, and she will be healed."

Jesus arrived at Jairus' house. Only Peter, James and John and Jairus and his wife were allowed to go in with Jesus. Everyone was howling and crying. "Stop crying!" Jesus ordered.

Jesus took the girl's hand and called out, "My child, get up." Life returned to the girl and she stood up at once. "Bring her something to eat," said Jesus.

Jesus showed his wonderful power over life and death and his care and concern for things like a little girl feeling hungry.

How glad she would have been to see her loving parents again and to see the Lord Jesus who had brought her back to life.

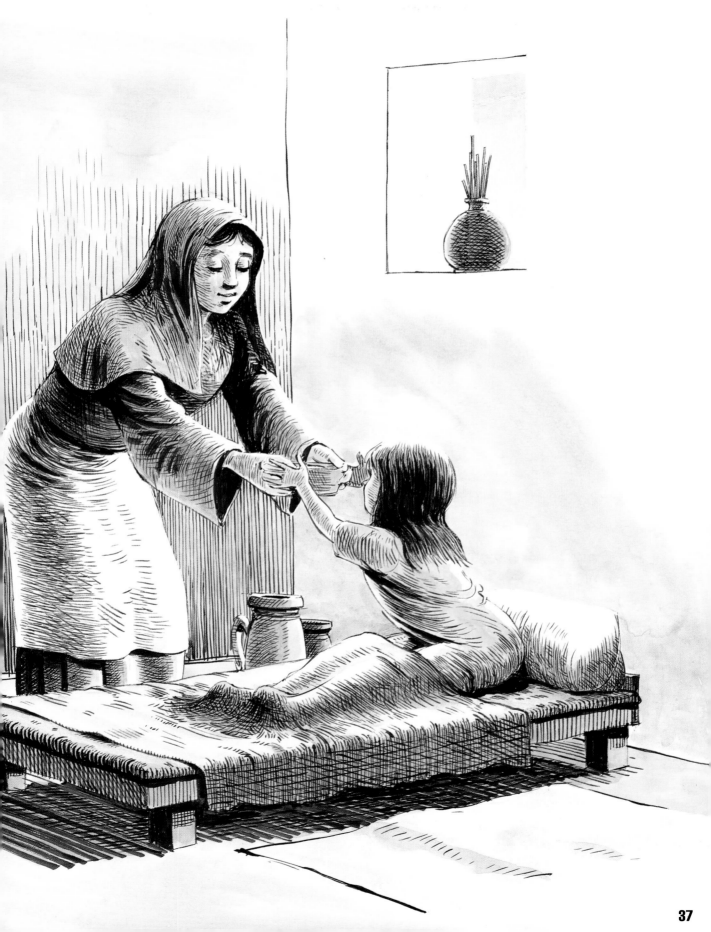

The Boy who gave his lunch to Jesus

John 6:1-15

A little boy went out with a small picnic lunch to spend the day in the country. He was among a large crowd of people who followed Jesus out of the town to listen to him preaching and teaching.

As the day passed the people became hungry. "Where could we buy enough bread to feed this crowd?" Jesus asked his disciple Philip.

"Even if we had plenty of money, we could hardly buy enough to give every one just one bite," replied Philip. Jesus already knew what he would do. Andrew came to Jesus and said, "There is a boy here who has five small barley loaves and two small fish. But how will they feed so many?"

"Tell the people to sit down on the grass," said Jesus. There was a huge crowd there, five thousand men as well as women and children, including the little boy with the picnic.

Jesus took the loaves, thanked God for them and broke them into pieces. He gave them to the disciples who handed them on to the people. He did the same with the fish. Jesus' power caused the food to multiply so that there was enough to feed that huge crowd of people. How pleased the little boy must have been that his picnic was used. The disciples gathered up the left-overs and filled twelve baskets!

Jesus
Loved Children

Matthew 18:1-9 & 19:13-15
& 21:12-16

The disciples asked Jesus the question, "Who is the greatest in the kingdom of heaven?"

To help them understand his answer, Jesus called a little child over to stand beside him. "Unless you become like a little child, you will never enter the kingdom of heaven," he said. "The greatest in the kingdom is the one who is as humble as this little child."

"The person who welcomes a little child like this one, is welcoming me," added Jesus.

Little children were brought by their parents to Jesus so that he would put his hands on them and pray for them.

The disciples were annoyed about this and tried to send them away. Perhaps they thought Jesus was too busy or that children were not important. Jesus thought differently.

"Let the little children come to me," he said. "Don't stop them. The kingdom of heaven belongs to them, and other children like them."

Jesus placed his hands on them and blessed them.

When Jesus came to Jerusalem to face his death on the cross, he rode on a donkey. Crowds went ahead and followed, shouting "Hosanna in the Highest."

When he reached the temple, he healed blind and lame people. The children gathered round and shouted praise to Jesus - "Hosanna to the Son of David!"

The officials were angry, but Jesus was pleased. He reminded them that it says in the Bible in the book of Psalms that children and infants would praise the Lord.

Timothy - A young missionary

Acts 16:1-5 &   1 & 2 Timothy

Timothy was brought up in Lystra. His mother was Jewish and his father was from Greece. His mother Eunice and his grandmother Lois loved and trusted God and they taught Timothy the ways of God from the Scriptures from his earliest years.

The Christian people in Lystra thought highly of Timothy. When Paul the missionary came to their town they told him all about Timothy.

Paul chose Timothy to be one of his assistants and to travel on his missionary journey with him.

He was sent on special trips to the church at Corinth and also to the church at Thessalonica in order to strengthen and encourage the Christians there. That was an important task for such a young man.

Timothy was not a very strong person and Paul advised him to take a little wine now and again as medicine to help his digestion.

Timothy was naturally timid but Paul encouraged him in his work of spreading the Gospel. He told him that training to be godly was far more important than physical training. Even though he was young, he had to set an example for the Christians. In the way he spoke and lived, he showed them love, his faith in God and the wish to be pure and holy.

Jesus - A special Baby

Matthew 1&2   Luke 1&2

We are told about many children in the Bible, but Jesus is the most special. His coming to this world was different from that of any other child. His mother Mary was told by an angel that she would have a son, called Jesus the Saviour. He had no natural human father. The power of God worked in Mary to produce the baby Jesus. This had been foretold many years before in the Bible. He would be called Immanuel which means 'God with us'. Jesus was the Son of God. This was explained to Joseph, Mary's husband and he took good care of Mary and brought up Jesus as his own son.

Jesus was born in Bethlehem in a poor rough stable because there was no room anywhere else. News of the birth of this special baby was given by an angel to shepherds watching over their flock of sheep. They were told that a Saviour was born - Christ the Lord. The shepherds hurried to Bethlehem and found Mary and Joseph and the baby Jesus. They spread the good news to all they knew, and praised·God for this wonderful child.

Wise men from the east also came to look for Jesus. They realised that he was the king of the Jews. They brought him precious gifts of gold, frankincense and myrrh. King Herod was angry at reports of a king of the Jews. He wanted to get rid of Jesus. He gave orders that all baby boys in and around Bethlehem should be killed.

But God had already warned Joseph in a dream to take Mary and Jesus away out of the country. They went to Egypt, well out of Herod's reach, where Jesus spent the first years of his life. After Herod died it was safe to go back to the land of Israel. The family went to the north, to Galilee and settled in the town of Nazareth. There Jesus grew strong and healthy and wise. He was like no other child. He did not sin but always did what God wanted him to do.

Jesus - A special Child

Luke 2:41-52

Every year Jesus' parents went to Jerusalem for the Feast of the Passover. When he was twelve, Jesus went too. After the Feast, the party from Nazareth returned home. Jesus stayed behind in Jerusalem on his own. Mary and Joseph assumed that Jesus was with other friends. After they had travelled for a day, they realised he was missing. Back they went to look for him. Jerusalem was a big city. They looked anxiously for three days before they found him in the temple. He was sitting with the teachers listening to them and asking questions. Everyone was amazed at his knowledge. Mary scolded him when she saw him. "Why did you do this? We have been so worried," she said. "Why were you searching for me?" he asked her. "Did you not know that I had to be in my Father's house?"

They did not understand that he meant God his Father. Jesus went back to Nazareth with them and was obedient to Mary and Joseph. He grew up to be strong and healthy in mind, body and spirit. God was pleased with him.

Children Today

God is interested in children today too. They are important to him.

The Lord Jesus came to the world to suffer and die, not only for old people, but also for children.

Jesus wants children today to do what they can for him. Perhaps you can tell somebody about the help that Jesus can give just as the servant girl told Naaman where he could get help. You can sing praise to God just as the children in Jerusalem did long ago. You can be willing to listen to God's word, the Bible, as Samuel listened to what God had to say. You can ask God to help you in difficulties as David did. The best thing that you can do for Jesus is to love him and to trust in him.

"From infancy you have known the holy Scriptures, which are able to make you wise for salvation through faith in Christ Jesus."

2 Timothy 3:15